How to Draw the Life and Times of
William McKinley

Lewis K. Parker

The Rosen Publishing Group's
PowerKids Press™
New York

This book is dedicated to my family, especially to Dakota, Tyrus, and Nicholas.

Published in 2006 by The Rosen Publishing Group, Inc.
29 East 21st Street, New York, NY 10010

First Edition

Editor: Melissa Acevedo
Layout Design: Julio A. Gil
Photo Researcher: Jeffrey Wendt

Illustrations: All illustrations by Holly Cefrey.
Photo Credits: pp. 4, 9, 14 Rosen Publishing Group; pp. 7, 12, 22, 24 (bottom) Library of Congress Prints and Photographs Division; p. 8 © Hulton/Archive/Getty Images; pp. 10, 16 © Corbis; p. 18 Library of Congress Rare Book and Special Collections Division; p. 20 (bottom) © Bettmann/Corbis; p. 24 (top) Courtesy, U.S. Naval Historical Center; p. 26 (top) © David J. & Janice L. Frent Collection/Corbis; p. 26 (bottom) Giraudon/Art Resource, NY; p. 28 The White House Collection, Courtesy the White House Historical Association.

Library of Congress Cataloging-in-Publication Data

Parker, Lewis K.
  How to draw the life and times of William McKinley / Lewis K. Parker.— 1st ed.
    p. cm. — (A kid's guide to drawing the presidents of the United States of America)
  Includes bibliographical references and index.
  ISBN 1-4042-3001-7 (library binding)
  1. McKinley, William, 1843–1901—Juvenile literature. 2. Presidents—United States–Biography—Juvenile literature. 3. Drawing—Technique—Juvenile literature. I. Title. II. Series.

  E711.6.P27 2006
  973.8'8'092—dc22

                              2005000069

Printed in China

Contents

The Path to the White House

William McKinley, the twenty-fifth president of the United States, was born on January 29, 1843, in Niles, Ohio. He was the seventh of nine children. When he was nine years old, his family moved to Poland, Ohio. It was here that he attended a private  school called the Poland Academy. He became president of the Poland Academy Debate Club and did very well in all his subjects. In 1860, McKinley entered Allegheny College in Meadville, Pennsylvania. After less than a year, he left Allegheny College and returned to Poland, Ohio, to work as a teacher and post office clerk.

Around this time slavery was becoming a major issue in America and dividing the country. Fearing slavery would be ended in America, southern states left the Union to form their own country. They called this country the Confederate States of America. The Civil War began when the Confederates attacked

Union-held Fort Sumter in South Carolina on April 12, 1861. McKinley immediately joined the 23rd Ohio Volunteer Infantry Regiment, which later became a part of the Union army. By the end of the war, in 1865, he had been moved up to the rank of major.

After the war McKinley returned to Ohio, where he studied to become a lawyer. In 1876, he was elected to the U.S. House of Representatives by the people of Ohio. He served six terms. In 1891, he was elected as governor of Ohio. In 1896, the Republican Party, which supported low taxes, nominated McKinley as their presidential candidate.

You will need the following supplies to draw the life and times of William McKinley:

✓ A sketch pad   ✓ An eraser   ✓ A pencil   ✓ A ruler

These are some of the shapes and drawing terms you need to know:

Horizontal Line	——	Squiggly Line	∿
Oval	⬭	Trapezoid	⏢
Rectangle	▭	Triangle	△
Shading	▰	Vertical Line		
Slanted Line	/	Wavy Line	∿

The Twenty-fifth U.S. President

William McKinley was inaugurated on March 4, 1897. By April the United States was involved in the Spanish-American War. At the time Spain controlled Cuba but the Cuban people were fighting for their independence. At first McKinley did not get involved. However, when Spain was accused of blowing up the U.S. battleship *Maine*, which was in the harbor of Havana, Cuba, he decided to take action. By August 1898, the United States had won the war. The treaty that ended the war gave Cuba independence and the United States control of Puerto Rico, Guam, and the Philippines. McKinley's popularity increased.

In 1900, McKinley was elected for a second term. During his first term, McKinley had dealt mainly with the relationships between the United States and other countries. During his second term, he planned to deal with problems within the United States. Before he could carry out his plans, he was shot by a man named Leon Czolgosz on September 6, 1901. President McKinley died on September 14, 1901.

This picture shows the newly sworn in president giving his inaugural speech. In his speech McKinley vowed that the United States would not enter any war until they had exhausted every method to keep peace. One of his goals as president was to avoid war at all costs.

William McKinley's Ohio

This house in Canton, Ohio, is where McKinley lived with his wife until 1891.

Ohio

Map of the United States of America

William McKinley's kin originally came to America from Scotland and Ireland. At first they settled in Pennsylvania, but they soon moved west to build farms in Ohio. In 1803, Ohio became the seventeenth state to enter the Union. Over the years Ohio became a magnet for settlers because of its good farmland. By 1830, more than 900,000 people lived there.

William McKinley lived in Ohio his whole life, and the state has found many ways to honor him. Visitors to Canton, Ohio, can tour the McKinley house. It is the house where McKinley's wife, Ida, grew up. She lived here with McKinley from 1878 to 1891. In 2000, the house was named as a First Ladies National Historic Site. The house was remodeled so that the patterns of wallpaper, carpets, and rugs are the same as they were when the McKinleys lived there.

His grave is located at the McKinley National Memorial, which is also in Canton, Ohio. More than two million bricks were used to build the memorial and 108 steps lead up to its entrance. A 23-foot (7-m) high bronze statue of McKinley stands halfway up the steps. The statue was sculpted based on a picture of McKinley giving his last speech. Inside the memorial are the graves of President McKinley, his wife, and their two children. The memorial is open to the public.

This picture of the McKinley National Memorial in Canton, Ohio, was taken in the early 1900s. Construction of the memorial began in 1905 and was completed in 1907.

The Childhood of William McKinley

In 1843, William McKinley was born in Niles, Ohio, in the house shown here. When he was old enough, McKinley started attending school in a one-room schoolhouse, where he learned reading, writing,

and arithmetic. When he was not in school, he was always helping out around the family farm. For fun he played baseball or marbles with other children. He was also very good with a bow and arrow and could hit nearly any target at which he aimed.

In 1852, McKinley's family moved to Poland, Ohio, so the children could get a better education. McKinley went to the Poland Academy. After he became president of the academy's debate club, he discovered that he enjoyed speaking before groups of people. In 1860, at the age of 17, McKinley attended Allegheny College in Meadville, Pennsylvania. He studied so hard that he became sick and had to return home after a few months. For the next year, he worked in Poland as a teacher and then as a clerk in the post office.

1

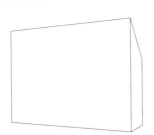

William McKinley was born in this house on January 29, 1843. This picture of the house was taken in 1902, shortly after his death. Begin the house by drawing a large rectangle. Draw the shape that connects to the right side of the rectangle.

2

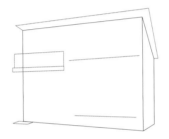

Use lines to create the roof shape as shown. Add two horizontal lines to the right side of the house as shown. These will be guidelines for the windows. Add the rectangular shapes to the left side of the house as shown. Add the shape at the base of the left side of the house.

3

Erase extra lines. Add lines to the roof as shown. Add four windows to the right side of the house using the guidelines from step 2. Add the door. Add lines to the rectangles from step 2. Draw curved lines around the base of the house for the ground.

4

Add a line to the roof for the trim. Add horizontal and vertical lines to the windows for detail. Add lines for the rails on the shape to the left. Add shapes to the door as shown. Add lines to the base of the house on the right and to the shape at the bottom left.

5

Erase all extra lines. Add shapes to the right side of the house as shown. Add more lines to the windows. Add shapes and lines to the door. Add more rails and a door to the shape on the left as shown. Add two vertical lines to the right side of the door.

6

Finish the drawing of the house by shading. Try to show the horizontal boards that make up the house. Keep in mind when shading that the doors of the house are darker than the rest of the house. Excellent work!

Serving in the Civil War

William McKinley's life changed in 1861, while he was working in Poland, Ohio. Slavery had become a major issue, and in 1861, 11 Southern states formed their own nation, called the Confederate States of America. Later that year the

Civil War began. In June 1861, McKinley joined the 23rd Ohio Volunteer Infantry Regiment, which later became part of the Union army. On September 17, 1862, he fought in the Battle of Antietam in Maryland, shown in the painting above. As bullets flew around him, McKinley drove a wagon of supplies to the soldiers using the Middle Bridge, shown at the top of the page. As a reward for his bravery, he was made second lieutenant. In 1864, McKinley was made brevet major when he risked his life a second time. McKinley went home to Ohio when the war ended in April 1865.

1

The picture of the Middle Bridge that appears on page 12 was taken soon after the Battle of Antietam. To begin drawing start with a large rectangle. Then draw a curved line across the rectangle as shown.

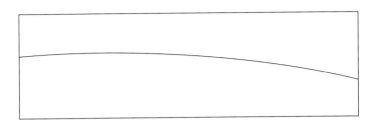

2

Draw another curved line above the line from step 1. Then draw three curved shapes below the first curved line as shown. These three shapes will be the arches of the bridge.

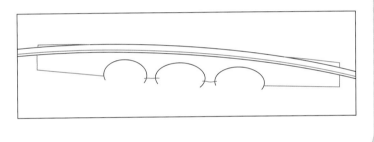

3

Use straight lines to draw the base on each side of the bridge. Add small lines between the arches. Draw vertical lines on either side of the bridge. At the top of these lines, add slanted lines that connect to the bridge. Add another curved line under the curved line from step 1.

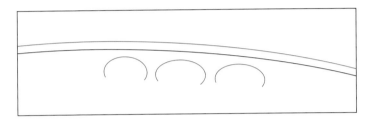

4

Erase extra lines. Draw the bumpy lines that begin at the bottom, pass through the arches, and extend to the top right. These lines will be the water. Add two shapes between the arches as shown. Fill them with rounded shapes. Add lines to either side of the bridge as shown.

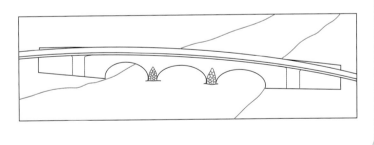

5

Add the reflection of the bridge to the water as shown. Finish the Middle Bridge by shading. Great work!

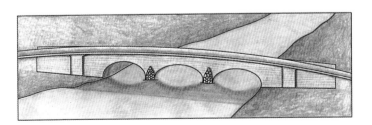

Life as a Lawyer

After returning to Ohio in 1865, William McKinley became a clerk in the law office of Charles Glidden in Youngstown, Ohio. In the fall of 1866, McKinley entered Albany Law School in Albany, New York. By March 1867, he thought he knew enough law to 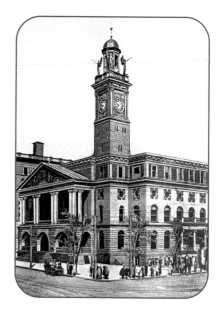 begin working as a lawyer. He returned to Ohio and passed the test that would allow him to practice law. He then opened his law office in Canton.

McKinley always carefully prepared for his cases. Because of this he won most of them. Judge George W. Belden thought McKinley did such a good job that he asked him to join his law firm, or a company made up of lawyers. By 1869, McKinley was a well-known and successful lawyer. He was elected as prosecuting attorney for Stark County, Ohio. A prosecuting attorney brings charges against people who break laws in that county. McKinley's office was now in the Stark County Courthouse, shown in the picture above.

1

This picture of the Stark County Courthouse is from the early 1900s. To draw the tower, begin with a rectangle. Add a long vertical line as shown. Add the shape at the base of the rectangle.

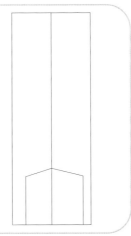

2

Add a bent line across the top of the shape as shown. Add a thin shape on top of the original shape from step 1. Then add another shape that looks like the original one.

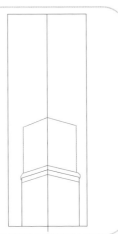

3

Add small rectangles for windows to the bottom. Use slanted lines to add the shape on top. Notice how some of the lines meet at points.

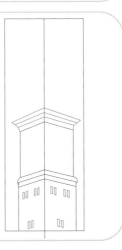

4

Add lines as shown to the shape from step 2. Add three more shapes to the top of the tower.

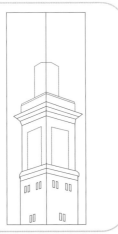

5

Draw two more shapes on top of the tower. Add three curved shapes as guides for the statues. Add lines for the rails as shown. Add circles and lines to the center of the tower as shown.

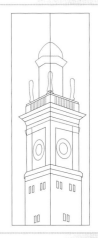

6

Add a line to the top of the tower. Draw the wings, arms, and heads of the statues. Add lines to their clothing. Add detail to the tower. Add small circles and hands to the clocks.

7

Draw two ovals on the line that extends from the tower. Add trumpets, more arms, and the bases to the statues. Add lines and curved shapes to the tower for detail.

8

Erase all extra lines. Finish the tower of the Stark County Courthouse with shading. Good job!

Ida Saxton McKinley

Soon after William McKinley became the prosecuting attorney in 1869, he met Ida Saxton at a town picnic in Canton. Ida's father, James Saxton, owned the First National Bank of Canton, where Ida worked. McKinley and Ida fell in love, and they married on January 25, 1871.  Ida's father gave the couple a house in Canton as a wedding present.

The McKinleys' first child, Katherine, was born on Christmas Day, 1871. Another daughter, named Ida, was born on April 1, 1873. The McKinleys were a happy couple. Then a series of sad events occurred. In early 1873, Ida's mother died. In August 1873, their daughter Ida died from a serious illness. Then in June 1876, their daughter Katherine died. These deaths caused Ida to become anxious and physically weak. She also began to suffer from epilepsy because of the anxiety she felt. The illness caused her to have fits in which she shook or fainted. McKinley took care of his wife for the rest of his life.

1 This picture of Ida Saxton McKinley is from 1900. Start by drawing a rectangle. Add two ovals for the guide to her head and hand. Add lines for the guide to her body.

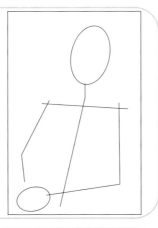

2 Add a curve to her head and an oval for the ear guide. Add the guides for her mouth, nose, and eyes. Draw the body outline. Add a curved line for her other hand.

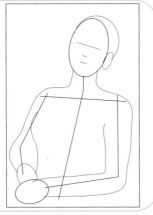

3 Erase the body guides from step 1. Draw Ida's eyebrows, eyes, nose, and mouth as shown. Draw her ear, cheek, and jaw as shown. Draw the collar on her dress. Add fingers to her hand.

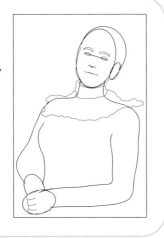

4 Erase all extra lines. Add small circles inside Ida's eyes. Add her hair as shown. Add lines around her nose and mouth as shown. Add detail to Ida's ear. Add fingers to her other hand. Draw the sleeves using squiggly lines.

5 Erase extra guides and lines. Add lines to her hair. Draw the chair behind her. Draw her eyelids. Add detail lines to her dress and the collar as shown.

6 Add squiggly lines in her hair for detail. Finish adding lines to her dress and collar as shown for detail. Add lines and an arm to her chair as shown. Add shapes to the chair for decoration.

7 Erase all extra lines. Finish your drawing of Ida Saxton McKinley by shading. Notice that certain parts of her dress are darker than others. Excellent work!

McKinley in Congress

Over time William McKinley became involved in politics. He was elected to the U.S. House of Representatives in 1876. He served for 12 years as the Ohio Republican representative. The Democratic legislature wanted McKinley out of Congress. They

knew that congressional representatives are elected from districts in their states, so in 1878, they changed the boundaries of the voting district. They did this so that McKinley's Democratic opponent would win. This practice became known as gerrymandering, as shown in the political cartoon above. McKinley campaigned hard and won the election.

In Congress McKinley supported a high tariff. A tariff is a tax on goods that are imported into the United States to be sold. He thought this tariff would protect American businesses. In 1890, Congress passed the McKinley Tariff Act. People became angry when the tariff did not work, and McKinley was not reelected in 1890.

1 This political cartoon shows the redrawing of district lines. Known as gerrymandering, this practice made reelection hard for opposing political party members. Draw a rectangle. Add a horizontal and vertical line that cross in the middle.

2 Draw an oval. This will be the guide for the gerrymander's head. Add a line with many angles in it as shown. This line will be the guide for the body.

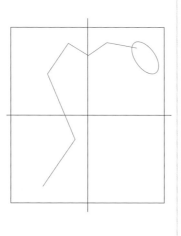

3 Draw the head and mouth inside the oval as shown. Use the guide to add the gerrymander's body. Create this form with curved and squiggly lines. Use the guidelines from step 1 to help you position the body outline correctly.

4 Erase the head and body guides. Draw the wing as shown. Draw the gerrymander's legs and feet using squiggly lines. Add teeth inside the mouth and a line for the tongue. Add a squiggly line on his head and a line for the eye.

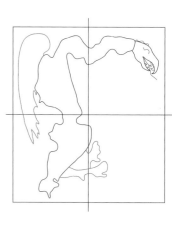

5 Erase extra lines, including the ones on his head. Add detail to his eye, nose, head, and tongue as shown. Add lines to the wing. Draw the lines across the body as shown. Add in his toes and claws.

6 Finish your drawing of the gerrymander with shading. His wings are darker than the rest of his body. Good work! What a great drawing!

McKinley as Governor of Ohio

Despite losing the congressional election in 1890, William McKinley remained active in politics. In 1892, he won the election for governor of Ohio. He served as governor for four years. It was around this time that he started to wear a carnation, as shown in the bottom picture here. He thought the carnation gave him good luck. Years later Ohio made the red carnation, shown above, the state's official flower in honor of McKinley. As governor, McKinley pushed for laws to make Ohio's railroads and factories safer for

workers. In 1894, coal miners in Ohio went on strike. They stopped trains and destroyed private property. McKinley reestablished peace by sending the National Guard. When he learned that the coal miners had gone on strike because their families were going hungry, he sent them trainloads of food and supplies.

1

To draw the red carnation, Ohio's state flower, begin with a shape that will be the base of the flower. Add a small circle underneath it. Draw the first petal using squiggly lines for the top part.

2

Erase the top part of the circle from step 1. Draw the stem as shown. Draw more petals as shown.

3

Erase any extra lines. Add a leaf to the right side of the base of the flower. Draw more petals as shown. Add a thinner stem to the bottom of the stem from step 2.

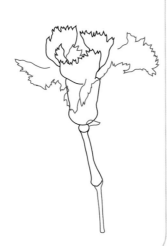

4

Erase extra lines in the petals. Add leaves to the smaller stem from step 3. Add another leaf to the base of the flower. Draw more petals as shown.

5

Erase extra lines in the leaves you just added. Draw a line on the stem. Draw more petals as shown. These extra petals are to make the carnation appear fuller.

6

Finish your carnation with shading. Notice that the stem and inner parts of the flower are darker. What a beautiful flower! Good job!

Running for President

In 1895, William McKinley decided not to seek reelection as governor of Ohio. He had his sights set on the presidency. He began campaigning and giving speeches. When the Republican Party met in St. Louis, Missouri, in 1896 to select their presidential candidate,

they chose McKinley. The Democratic Party chose William Jennings Bryan as McKinley's opponent.

Bryan traveled more than 18,000 miles (28,968 km) across the United States to campaign. He spoke out against a high tariff. He was also against basing the value of paper money on gold. McKinley knew he could not compete with Bryan's tireless campaign. He chose to stay at home and give speeches from the front porch of his home in Canton. McKinley supported a high tariff. He was also for basing the value of paper money on gold. More than 750,000 people went to hear his campaign speeches. The poster shown above is from the 1896 presidential campaign.

1

To draw McKinley's 1896 presidential campaign poster, which is shaped like a shield, start with a large rectangle. Draw a vertical line down the center.

2

Use the guides to draw the top of the shield. Draw the bottom of the shield. The bottom is made with two curved lines that meet at a point at the bottom of the rectangle.

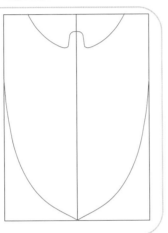

3

Erase most of the rectangle as shown. Draw a horizontal line across the shield. Draw two ovals as shown. Inside each oval draw a smaller one as shown.

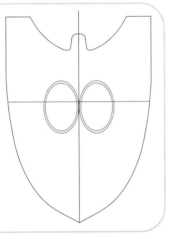

4

Erase part of the horizontal line. Add the head guides inside the ovals. Add a curved line to the guides for their necks and shoulders. Add horizontal and vertical lines as shown.

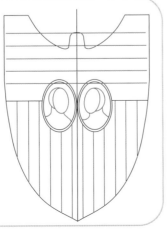

5

Erase extra lines. Add stars on the top part of the shield using the horizontal lines. Begin the banner over the people. Add the hairlines, cheeks, jaws, eyes, noses, and mouths.

6

Erase extra lines. Add more stars. Add lines and the word "PROTECTION" to the banner. Finish the faces. Add lines to the ears. Add their collars. Add a bow tie to the left figure.

7

Erase extra lines. Write the words "AND" and "SOUND MONEY" on the banner. Add lines to the banner. Draw the rest of the clothes. Finish the mouth. Add the mustache.

8

Erase extra lines. Finish the shield with shading. McKinley is on the left. His vice-presidential running mate, Garrett Hobart, is on the right. Well done!

President McKinley's First Term

William McKinley won the 1896 election and took office on March 4, 1897. As president he wanted peaceful relations with other countries. Unfortunately, America was soon swept up in the Spanish-American War. At the time Cuba was fighting Spain for independence. McKinley did

not want to get involved. He was forced to take action when Spain was accused of blowing up the U.S. battleship *Maine*, shown above, which was in the harbor of Havana, Cuba. On April 25, 1898, the United States went to war with Spain. The picture above shows a battle fought on June 11, 1898. The war ended in 1899. Cuba won its independence. The United States was given Puerto Rico, Guam, and the Philippine Islands, all formerly held by Spain. McKinley had helped gain land for America.

1

To begin drawing the *Maine,* start by drawing the shape that will become the body of the boat. Add a squiggly line as shown for the water.

2

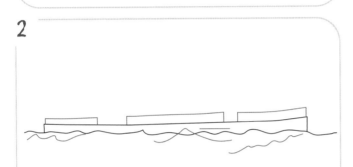

Draw nine straight lines to create rectangular shapes on the body of the boat as shown. Draw more squiggly lines in the water. Add a short line to the body of the boat as shown.

3

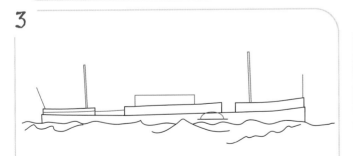

Erase extra lines. Add flagpoles as shown. Draw two poles that come out from the other rectangular shapes. Add a rectangular shape on top of the middle one. Draw a curved line on the short line from step 2. Draw a horizontal line on the left side of the boat.

4

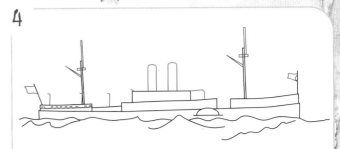

Erase extra lines. Draw two curved shapes for steam pipes in the middle of the boat. Add a shape to the rectangular shape from step 3. Add flags to the flagpoles. Add shapes to the other poles. Add windows to the left side of the boat. Add lines coming from the boat.

5

Erase extra lines in the shapes you added to the masts. Draw steam coming out from the pipes. Add more lines to the poles. Add the shapes to the boat as shown. Add a square to the flag on the left as shown.

6

Erase any extra lines. Finish the boat by shading carefully. What a great job!

The Death of President McKinley

In 1900, William McKinley ran for a second term as president. McKinley gave a few speeches from his front porch in Canton. His campaign slogan was, "Four Years More of the Full Dinner Pail" as shown on the button on the right. McKinley won the election and was inaugurated on March 4, 1901. Soon after McKinley decided to tour the southern and western states.

In September 1901, McKinley attended the Pan-American Exposition in Buffalo, New York. Some of America's newest inventions, including the automobile and the telephone, were being shown there. On September 6, the president stood greeting visitors to the exposition. One of the visitors, a man named Leon Czolgosz, had a gun. When McKinley went to shake his hand, Czolgosz fired two shots at him, as shown in the painting above. McKinley died eight days later on September 14, 1901.

1

To begin drawing the campaign button McKinley used in his 1900 presidential campaign, start with a large circle. Draw a smaller circle inside that one as shown.

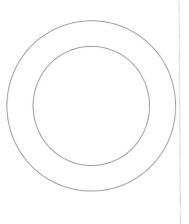

2

Draw the shape of the bottom of the dinner pail as shown. Write "McKINLEY" on the left side of the button. Add a small line underneath the lowercase C. Write "AND" in the top middle of the button.

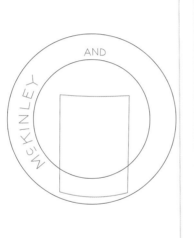

3

Erase the part of the circle that goes through the pail. Draw the top of the pail. Draw slightly curved horizontal lines on the pail. Add two small curves near the ends of the top line. Add "ROOSEVELT" on the right side of the button.

4

Start the pail's handle as shown. Add six more lines to the dinner pail. Write "FOUR" at the top of the dinner pail as shown. Write "YEARS MORE" and "OF THE" on the pail as shown.

5

Finish the handle by adding a shape to the top. Draw the curve near the top of the pail. Write "FULL DINNER PAIL" at the bottom of the pail as shown.

6

Erase extra lines. Finish the button with shading. The background behind the pail is very dark. Fill in the words "FULL DINNER PAIL" so that they are as dark as the background. You are done!

The People's President

In 1901, a train took William McKinley's body to Washington, D.C. This way Americans could pay their respects before he was taken to Ohio for burial. Thousands of people visited their president for a final time in the Capitol. The whole nation

mourned the loss of such a great man and president.

William McKinley gave America an important part of its history. He helped the United States become a major world power. Even though he was against the idea of war, he led America to victory in the Spanish-American War. He also opened the door for friendlier relations between America and other nations. McKinley did all he could to try and make life easier on poor people. That is why he believed that companies should pay more taxes. His humble background and friendly attitude allowed all ordinary people to like and to respect him. William McKinley was truly the people's president.

1

This picture of William McKinley was painted by Charles Ayer Whipple. To start draw a large rectangle. Add lines for the body guide. Add oval guides for the hands and head.

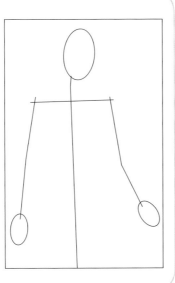

2

Draw a curved line on his head. Draw an oval guide for his ear. Draw lines for the guides to McKinley's eyes, nose, and mouth. Draw the outline of his body as shown.

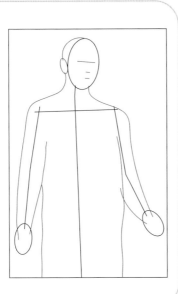

3

Erase the body guides. Draw ovals for his eyes using the guideline. Start his nose and mouth. Outline his ear. Draw his cheek, jaw, and chin as shown. Begin to draw his clothes and collar.

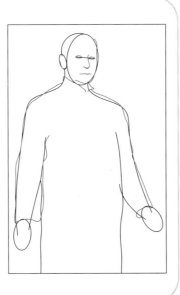

4

Erase extra lines in his head, face, and body. Draw his eyebrows and the circles in his eyes. Finish drawing his mouth and his nose. Draw his hair. Add detail to his ear as shown. Finish drawing his collar. Add lines for the coat. Draw his cuffs and fingers as shown.

5

Erase extra lines. Add dots to his eyes. Add lines to his face. Finish adding his clothing. Draw the paper in his left hand. Add glasses to his right hand. Add lines for thumbnails.

6

Erase the rest of the body guidelines. Erase the line of the paper that goes through McKinley's thumb. Finish your drawing with shading. You did an excellent job!

Timeline

1843 William McKinley is born in Niles, Ohio, on January 29.

1852 McKinley's family moves to Poland, Ohio, where he attends a private school called Poland Academy.

1860 At the age of 17, McKinley enrolls in Allegheny College.

1861 After a few months, McKinley is forced to leave Allegheny College. He returns home to Poland where he teaches and works as a clerk in the Poland post office.

The Civil War begins and in June, McKinley joins the 23rd Ohio Volunteer Infantry Regiment.

1862 William McKinley's regiment becomes part of the Union army in June.

1865 McKinley leaves the army and returns to Ohio to become a lawyer.

1867 William McKinley opens his law practice in Canton, Ohio.

1869 McKinley is elected prosecuting attorney for Stark County, Ohio.

1871 Ida Saxton and McKinley are married.

1876 McKinley is elected to the U.S. House of Representatives.

1890 To protect American businesses, McKinley proposes the McKinley Tariff.

1892 McKinley is elected governor of Ohio.

1896 McKinley is nominated as the Republican candidate for president.

1897 On March 4, McKinley is inaugurated as the twenty-fifth president of the United States of America.

1898 The United States fights Spain in the Spanish-American War. In the treaty that follows the war, the United States is given control of Puerto Rico, Guam, and the Philippines. Cuba gains independence.

1900 McKinley is reelected president of the United States.

1901 On September 6, McKinley is shot. He later dies on September 14.

Glossary

campaigned (kam-PAYND) Planned to get a certain result, such as to win an election.

candidate (KAN-dih-dayt) A person who runs in an election.

Civil War (SIH-vul WOR) The war fought between the Northern and the Southern states of America from 1861 to 1865.

Confederate States of America (kun-FEH-duh-ret STAYTS UV uh-MER-ih-kuh) A group of 11 Southern states that declared themselves separate from the United States from 1860 until 1861.

debate (dih-BAYT) Having to do with arguing or discussing.

epilepsy (EH-puh-lep-see) A brain disorder that causes sudden attacks like jerking or loss of consciousness.

imported (im-PORT-ed) Brought from another country for sale or use.

inaugurated (ih-NAW-gyuh-rayt-ed) Sworn into office.

infantry (IN-fun-tree) A group of men in the military.

involved (in-VOLVD) Kept busy by something.

lawyer (LOY-er) A person who gives advice about the law and who speaks for people in court.

legislature (LEH-jis-lay-chur) A body of people that has the power to make or pass laws.

nominated (NAH-mih-nayt-ed) To have suggested that someone or something should be given an award or a position.

opponent (uh-POH-nent) A person or a group that is against another.

politics (PAH-lih-tiks) The science of governments and elections.

regiment (REH-juh-ment) A group in the military.

site (SYT) The place where a certain event happens.

Union (YOON-yun) The Northern states that stayed with the federal government during the Civil War.

volunteer (vah-lun-TEER) Having to do with soldiers who had jobs outside the military before the war.

Index

Web Sites

Due to the changing nature of Internet links, PowerKids Press has developed an online list of Web sites related to the subject of this book. This site is updated regularly. Please use this link to access the list:
www.powerkidslinks.com/kgdpusa/mckinley/